NEURO LINGUISTIC PROGRAMMING

A Complete Guide For Empowering Communication And Navigating Life's Challenges For Personal Growth

WALTER ZYAIRE

No part of this book may be reproduced, stored in a retrieval system, or transmitted in any form or by any means, electronic, mechanical, photocopying, recording, or otherwise, without the express written permission of the author, with the exception of small extracts in critical reviews or articles.

DISCLAIMER

The information in this book is intended only for general informational purposes; it should not be used in lieu of professional advice or medical care. Since the author is not licensed to practice therapy, the information offered should not be used in place of the expertise, judgment, or guidance of qualified mental health or medical professionals. Readers are encouraged to consult therapists, medical specialists, or other qualified authorities regarding their particular situation and needs. The publisher and author disclaim all liability for any actions or decisions taken by readers based on the information in this book. Results may vary from person to person and this book's approaches, procedures, and strategies may not be suitable in all circumstances. Considering unique situations and consulting a qualified expert are essential when choosing the right course of action. Neither the publisher nor the author recommend or guarantee the efficacy of any therapy or treatment that is indicated in this book. Because the information is based on the author's research and understanding at the time of publishing, it could not reflect the most recent developments or practices in the treatment area. The publisher and the author both disclaim all liability for the accuracy, completeness, or use of the material in this book. Readers bear full responsibility for the decisions and actions they choose in light of the information presented in this book.

TABLE OF CONTENTS

ABOUT THE BOOK

"Neuro-linguistic Programming" is a book that provides readers with a thorough overview of the concepts, techniques, and various applications of NLP. It is a comprehensive handbook that explores the nuances of the field. The book presents the idea of natural language processing (NLP) in its introduction, outlining its history and development and stressing its general significance and wide range of applications across multiple domains.

The foundation is laid "Foundations of NLP," which clarifies the mind-body link and several fundamental concepts, such as representational systems, rapport building, calibrating, and anchoring. For readers to understand the essence of the NLP techniques and strategies covered throughout the book, this chapter acts as a vital building block.

Further exploration of particular facets of NLP, including assumptions, neurology, linguistics, methods, and modeling, is provided.

The book uses neurology and linguistics to show the complexities of the mind and language in NLP and it clarifies the power of positive presuppositions for bringing about transformation. The strategies and modeling chapter explains how people can develop and apply successful personal and professional models.

"NLP Techniques," offers a helpful overview of several NLP approaches, such as parts integration, six-step reframing, the swish pattern, visualizations, and sub modalities. These methods give readers practical tools for growth and transformation on a personal level.

The use of NLP in communication, personal growth, and a variety of domains including business, education, counseling, therapy, and everyday life is examined in the ensuing chapters. The book highlights linguistic patterns, persuasive techniques, and the growth of influence and persuasion, demonstrating how NLP may be a potent instrument in influencing interpersonal and professional relationships.

The book discusses NLP ethics, stressing the need for respect and consent as well as the obligations of practitioners. The book also covers NLP's future tendencies, emphasizing new developments in the field's research as well as its nexus with technology and upcoming applications.

This book is an invaluable tool for anyone looking for a thorough grasp of neuro-linguistic programming. Along with providing readers with useful tools, it also examines the ethical implications and potential directions for the developing field of NLP.

CHAPTER ONE

OVERVIEW OF NEURO-LINGUISTIC PROGRAMMING

NEURO-LINGUISTIC PROGRAMMING (NLP): WHAT IS IT?

A multifaceted method for comprehending and controlling human behavior, communication, and cognitive processes is called neuro-linguistic programming, or NLP. It includes a collection of methods and ideas that investigate the connections between language (linguistic), neurology (neuro), and experience-based behavioral patterns (programming). NLP was created in the 1970s by Richard Bandler and John Grinder, and it is influenced by several disciplines, including linguistics, cognitive psychology, and cybernetics. The basic idea behind NLP is that language, acquired behavioral patterns from experience, and brain functions are all connected. Through comprehending and directing these associations, people can improve their abilities to communicate, get over self-limiting ideas, and succeed both personally and professionally.

THE DEVELOPMENT AND HISTORY OF NLP

The origins and development of Neuro-linguistic Programming can be found in the partnership between linguist and Professor John Grinder and psychology student Richard Bandler. In their early work, they observed and imitated the communication patterns and behavioral patterns of effective therapists, including Virginia Satir, a well-known family therapist, and Fritz Perls, the founder of Gestalt therapy. Bandler and Grinder discovered important tactics and methods that worked well in achieving their goals through this modeling process. As a result, NLP was created and rapidly became well-known for its pragmatic and goal-oriented approach to communication and personal growth.

NLP has developed and broadened over time as a result of the innovative concepts and methods that its practitioners have brought to the discipline. Because of its adaptability, NLP has been used in a variety of contexts, such as business, education, therapy, and coaching. NLP has been applied in a variety of contexts, including sports coaching, sales and marketing, leadership development, and even therapy settings where it has been used to treat trauma, anxiety, and phobias. Different schools of thought have emerged within NLP as a result of its progress, each having its applications and viewpoints.

NLP'S SIGNIFICANCE AND USES

The potential of neuro-linguistic programming to enable people to comprehend and change their thought and behavior patterns is what makes it so significant. NLP helps people reach their goals and overcome limiting beliefs by giving them useful skills for goal-setting, successful communication, and personal transformation. Furthermore, because of its versatility, NLP is a useful tool for improving leadership, negotiating, and interpersonal skills in a variety of professional domains. Beyond personal growth, NLP is also used for organizational success. Here, it is used to enhance team dynamics, business communication, and even the formulation of more persuasive marketing messaging.

Neuro-linguistic programming is a strong and adaptable method for comprehending and modifying human behavior. Its development over time reflects a dynamic field that keeps evolving and adapting, incorporating ideas from many academic fields to improve its methods. The useful applications of NLP across a variety of industries demonstrate the field's significance and give people and organizations important resources for both career and personal success. In the fields of education, business, or therapy, NLP is still a useful tool for those who want to reach their full potential and make a lasting difference.

CHAPTER TWO

NLP'S FOUNDATIONS

RECOGNIZING THE LINK BETWEEN MIND AND BODY

A key idea in neuro-linguistic programming (NLP) is the mind-body connection, which highlights the complex interplay between our mental, emotional, and physical experiences. According to NLP, there is a bidirectional exchange of influences between the mind and body.

People can get insight into how their mental states affect their physiological reactions and vice versa by realizing and comprehending this link. NLP practitioners frequently investigate how internal representations, sensory perception, and linguistic patterns shape mental and physical well-being. Through addressing the interconnectedness of the mind and body, NLP seeks to enable people to make positive changes in their lives.

FUNDAMENTALS OF NLP

NLP's strategies and methodology are guided by a set of fundamental concepts that form their foundation. The notion that people can transform themselves for the better is one of the fundamental tenets. This premise supports the idea that individuals may change their attitudes, actions, and feelings for the better. The significance of sensory perception and subjective experience in forming an individual's world is a further fundamental premise. NLP highlights how language and communication impact these subjective experiences while acknowledging the individuality of each viewpoint. Furthermore, the notion of rapport—which will be covered in more detail later—is essential to promoting clear and efficient communication.

DEVELOPING A RAPPORT

A fundamental idea in NLP, rapport building is the development of a cordial and sympathetic relationship between people. It entails fostering an atmosphere of mutual respect, trust, and understanding since these things promote productive collaboration and communication. Mirroring and matching are two common NLP strategies for developing rapport. In these strategies, the practitioner gently matches their actions, like as body language and voice tone, with those of the other person. NLP seeks to build rapport to foster an atmosphere that is favorable to candid dialogue and teamwork, which in turn increases the possibility of successful outcomes in a variety of interpersonal situations.

ADJUSTMENT

Within NLP, calibration is the process of fine-tuning one's sensory acuity to pick up on nonverbal clues and minor behavioral changes in other people. The significance of being aware of the subtleties of tone, posture, gestures, and facial expressions is emphasized by NLP practitioners. People can learn about others' emotional states, ideas, and reactions by accurately calibrating.

By properly tailoring their communication and treatments, practitioners can promote better understanding and connection with those they contact thanks to this increased awareness.

SECURING

An effective NLP technique called "anchoring" is connecting a certain stimulus to a certain emotional or mental state. The underlying premise of this procedure is that people can access and generate desired states by activating related anchors. To create anchors, NLP practitioners employ a variety of sensory stimuli, including touch, visual cues, and audio signals.

An anchor can be utilized to subsequently elicit the positive emotions connected to a nice interaction, such as a kind touch on the shoulder during that chat. By enabling people to more deliberately control their emotional states and reactions, anchoring promotes both interpersonal and personal growth.

THE SYSTEM OF REPRESENTATION

The representational system in NLP describes how people mentally represent and process information from their outside world. The three main representational systems recognized by NLP are kinesthetic, auditory, and visual. Kinesthetic people emphasize feelings and bodily experiences, auditory people process information through sound and language, and visual people rely on visual images and signals. Determining a person's main representational system might provide important information about their decision-making, communication, and learning preferences. By conforming to the person's preferred representational system, NLP procedures use this knowledge to improve communication and foster greater understanding and connection in a variety of circumstances.

CHAPTYER THREE

NLP ASSUMPTIONS

NLP BELIEFS AND ASSUMPTIONS

As practitioners of Neuro-Linguistic Programming (NLP) are aware of the enormous influence that beliefs and assumptions have on an individual's perception, behavior, and overall experience, they place a high value on investigating these cognitive factors. According to NLP, each person has a distinct set of beliefs that have been influenced by their upbringing, culture, and personal values. Whether they are restrictive or empowering, these ideas have a major role in influencing how one experiences life. NLP places a strong emphasis on the identification and modification of limiting beliefs as a means of promoting positive transformation and personal development.

NLP acknowledges that people create their subjective realities by selectively deleting, manipulating, and filtering information. Beliefs and presumptions shape these filters, giving each person a different perspective on the world. NLP practitioners may assist people in widening their perspectives and reframing their ideas by recognizing and comprehending these filters, which will help them approach problems with a more creative mentality. The capacity to alter constrictive ideas and install empowering ones in their stead can be revolutionary, leading to a more positive and contented approach to living.

THE PERCEPTION POWER

The idea that reality is shaped by perception is fundamental to NLP. Realizing that people react to their subjective interpretation of reality rather than the actual reality itself is the key to understanding the power of perception. According to NLP, people may change how they see things by altering the internal representations they make of them. To change unfavorable perceptions into favorable ones, practitioners collaborate with clients to examine and alter the sensory representations—auditory, visual, and kinesthetic—that are connected to certain memories or circumstances.

NLP acknowledges that perception is flexible and changeable, offering a path for growth and conquering obstacles. Through the use of strategies like anchoring and reframing, people can change how they view the past and lessen the emotional impact of painful memories. This change in perspective enables people to tackle challenges both now and in the future with a more resilient and upbeat outlook.

MAKING USE OF POSITIVE PRESUPPOSITIONS TO EFFECT CHANGE

Good presuppositions are the cornerstone of NLP; they are powerful presumptions that point practitioners and clients in the direction of good development. These suppositions include the notions that there is no such thing as failure—only feedback—that people make the best decisions they can at any given moment and that everyone possesses the inner resources necessary to accomplish their goals. NLP practitioners provide a constructive, encouraging framework for assisting personal growth by accepting these positive presuppositions.

Positive presuppositions are a powerful tool in NLP because they help people think creatively and with possibilities. Individuals are encouraged to adopt more effective tactics and explore new perspectives to achieve their desired objectives by emphasizing their skills, resources, and potential for growth. This upbeat and forward-thinking strategy creates the conditions for a cooperative journey toward personal growth, enabling people to discover their innate potential and bring about long-lasting, beneficial change in their lives.

CHAPTER FOUR

NLP'S NEUROLOGY AND LINGUISTICS

BRAIN MAPPING: NEUROSCIENCE IN NLP

The field of neuro-linguistic programming, or NLP, explores the complex interplay between language and neurology to comprehend and modify human behavior. Fundamentally, NLP investigates the relationship between brain activity, linguistic patterns, and behavioral consequences to map the mind.

This multidisciplinary approach uses knowledge from neurology to understand how language shapes cognitive patterns and how the brain processes information.

The brain is viewed as a sophisticated information-processing system in the context of NLP. Educating practitioners on the neurological processes behind perception, memory, and decision-making enables them to create more successful language interventions.

NLP techniques frequently make use of neurology to generate patterns that mesh well with the brain's inherent functions, promoting behavior change and communication. Aiming to improve their capacity to connect neurologically with others, NLP practitioners map neural connections and comprehend sensory modalities.

LANGUAGE AS A MODAL TOOL

Language is an effective instrument for influencing feelings, changing behavior, and forming impressions. According to NLP, language is a dynamic force that may be used to create beneficial changes in addition to being a tool for communication. NLP practitioners may help people think differently, get rid of limiting ideas, and move toward their goals by using precise language patterns and deliberate word choices.

According to NLP, language plays a crucial role in the creation of subjective reality. Language used by people has a significant impact on how they understand and communicate their experiences. Through the analysis of linguistic patterns, nonverbal pragmatic psychologists can detect and alter ingrained cognitive habits, allowing people to reinterpret their experiences and take on more powerful viewpoints. This linguistic approach to change highlights the role that language plays in forming cognitive maps and affecting how people see and react to their environment.

LINGUISTICS: META-MODEL AND MILTON MODEL

Two essential linguistic frameworks in NLP with different applications in communication and change work are the Milton Model and the Meta-Model. Based on the research of linguist Noam Chomsky, the Meta-Model seeks to address communication distortions by revealing underlying thought processes through the specification and clarification of language. It serves as a precise instrument to extract more information and highlight assumptions, generalizations, and omissions that occur in language.

On the other hand, the Milton Model, which bears the name of the well-known hypnotist Milton H. Erickson, approaches language in a more liberal and creatively ambiguous manner. This approach uses indirection, metaphor, and ambiguity on purpose to get beyond conscious opposition and reach the unconscious mind. The Milton Model is frequently used in therapeutic settings to stimulate the unconscious mind's sensitivity to suggestion, create trance-like experiences, and promote creative thought.

The Milton Model and the Meta-Model show how linguistic structures can be used in NLP to analyze and alter communication for different goals, such as using deliberate vagueness to bring about transformative change or precise inquiry to clarify comprehension. These language aids greatly increase the efficiency of NLP methods in promoting both professional and personal growth.

CHAPTER FIVE

NLP MODELS AND STRATEGIES

EXERCISING EXCELLENCE MODELING

The goal of modeling excellence in natural language processing (NLP) is to create and apply models that aim to mimic remarkable language performance. To facilitate processes like language production, translation, and interpretation, these models try to replicate the subtleties and complexity of human language.

Mastering NLP modeling demands a thorough comprehension of context, linguistic structures, and the capacity to generalize over a wide range of linguistic patterns. To build models that perform exceptionally well in a range of NLP tasks, researchers and practitioners frequently utilize methods like transformers and deep learning, demonstrating their dedication to superior language representation.

DEVELOPING AND PUTTING INTO PRACTICE A STRATEGY

In the field of NLP, developing and implementing strategies entails carefully organizing and carrying out methods to deal with particular language-related problems. To select the best model architectures, training approaches, and data preprocessing strategies, researchers and developers must plan.

To get the best outcomes, implementing these tactics frequently necessitates iterative cycles of experimenting, fine-tuning, and evaluation. To improve the general efficacy of NLP applications, other tactics could include utilizing transfer learning, domain-specific modifications, or pre-trained models.

The creation of reliable and effective NLP systems depends on the successful formulation and use of strategies.

BUILDING BOTH INDIVIDUAL AND EXPERT MODELS

NLP's creation of personal and professional models is concerned with the frameworks that direct both individual and group approaches to language processing. Researchers and practitioners frequently build mental models and frameworks for comprehending language phenomena on a personal level, which directs their investigation of cutting-edge methods and paradigms.

These individual models influence how people approach issues, formulate research questions, and analyze findings. Professionally speaking, businesses can create models for NLP initiatives that include standards for model development and implementation, ethical considerations, and best practices. The development and observance of clear personal and professional models are essential to the general prosperity and moral conduct of NLP practitioners.

CHAPTER SIX

NLP METHODS

IMAGES & VISUALIZATIONS

In Natural Language Processing (NLP), visualizations and imagery are essential. This method entails constructing mental scenarios or images to improve cognitive functions and accomplish particular goals. NLP practitioners frequently teach clients to vividly see desired situations or results to maximize the mind's ability to affect attitudes and actions.

Visualizations are useful in many situations, including goal-setting, conquering obstacles, and developing optimistic outlooks. NLP practitioners hope to enhance personal and professional development by utilizing imagery and visualizations to access the mind's capacity to form and react to mental images.

SUBMODALITIES

In NLP parlance, sub modalities are the finer points of differentiation within sensory experiences. These intangible components—visual, aural, kinesthetic, olfactory, and gustatory—all play a part in how a person perceives a given event. NLP practitioners may recognize and control the sensory components linked to memories or thoughts by comprehending sub modalities. People can effectively modify their emotional reactions, shift limiting beliefs, and improve pleasant experiences by doing this. Sub modality inquiry is essential to NLP therapy because it helps people reframe their experiences and accomplish their goals.

SWISH DESIGN

An NLP approach called the Swish Pattern is used to break undesirable thought patterns or behaviors and swap them out for more constructive ones. It entails forming an image in your mind of the undesirable behavior and quickly substituting it with a more positive vision. By quickly alternating between these mental representations, the intention is to rewire the mind so that positive behavior is more tempting and negative behavior is less appealing. The Swish Pattern provides a methodical approach to behavioral change within the NLP framework and is frequently used to address habits, anxieties, or self-limiting beliefs.

SIX-STEP REWORDING

An NLP approach called Six-Step Reframing helps resolve internal conflicts by bringing disparate aspects of a person's mind into harmony. To create a solution that meets the needs of all parties, this method entails first recognizing and comprehending the good intentions underlying each opposing component. By recognizing and valuing the constructive intention underlying seemingly incompatible components, people can attain internal coherence and mitigate internal discord. In the framework of NLP treatments, the Six-Step Reframing technique is used to improve self-awareness, foster internal harmony, and enable personal growth.

QUICK CURE FOR PHOBIAS

An NLP method called "Fast Phobia Cure" is intended to swiftly address and eliminate phobias. With this method, the experience is mentally detached from the emotional charge corresponding to phobic stimuli. People can reframe their reactions to the feared stimulus by changing the sensory elements and mental spatial representation of the phobia. The Quick Phobia Cure is well known for its effectiveness in offering quick relief from phobias, adding to the NLP therapeutic toolset for conquering unreasonable fears and worries.

CHAPTER SEVEN

NLP IN INTERACTION

PROFICIENCY IN COMMUNICATION

The ability to communicate effectively is essential for negotiating the challenging terrain of interpersonal relationships. It includes a variety of verbal and non-verbal clues in addition to verbal communication. For example, active listening is an essential component in which people can comprehend the underlying intentions and feelings in addition to just hearing what is spoken. Furthermore, a clear and succinct manner of thinking also adds to the effectiveness of communication. To promote understanding and connection, both verbal and nonverbal cues, such as tone of voice and body language, are crucial.

LANGUAGE PATTERNS' POWER

In the fields of communication and natural language processing, the Power of Language Patterns is crucial.

Language patterns are the organized ways in which words and phrases are used to effectively communicate ideas. People can shape how information is perceived and how a message is interpreted by using language strategies. This entails speaking positively, structuring information in a way that appeals to the audience, and using metaphors to improve understanding. Knowing language patterns gives communicators the ability to create engaging stories and modify their messages to get the desired results.

ESTABLISHING AND SUSTAINING RAPPORT

One of the most important components of good communication is establishing and preserving rapport. The development of a peaceful and constructive relationship between people is known as rapport. It entails establishing a relationship based on mutual respect, trust, and understanding. NLP approaches can be used to improve rapport-building behaviors like matching and mirroring, which include matching the other person's behavior.

Developing a rapport facilitates open communication, which in turn facilitates the resolution of disputes, cooperation, and the accomplishment of common goals.

CONVINCING AND INFLUENCING

Strong communication instruments that have the power to sway beliefs and motivate behavior are persuasion and influence. NLP techniques help us comprehend how others can be influenced by our language and communication habits. Persuasive language, narrative, and emotional appeal are powerful tools for changing people's minds and inspiring them to do certain things. But when it comes to persuasion, ethical issues take center stage, underscoring how crucial it is to use these abilities sensibly and openly. Understanding the audience, their values, and the context of the communication is crucial to mastering the art of persuasion.

NLP in communication takes a multimodal approach, with the cornerstone being Effective Communication

Skills. While Establishing and Sustaining Rapport fosters an atmosphere that is favorable for candid communication, the Power of Language Patterns enables the strategic transmission of messages. Ultimately, when used appropriately, persuasion and influence can be effective instruments for attaining favorable results in a range of personal and professional contexts.

CHAPTER EIGHT

NLP IN SELF-DEVELOPMENT

OBJECTIVE SETTING AND ACHIEVING

When it comes to personal growth, goal-setting is a crucial notion that helps people live lives that are more purposeful and rewarding. Setting and achieving objectives can be better understood and optimized with the help of NLP (Neuro-Linguistic Programming). Through the application of NLP techniques, people can improve their goal-setting strategies by gaining a deeper comprehension of their cognitive processes, language usage, and behavioral inclinations. NLP encourages people to clearly describe their objectives and to use sensory-rich language that helps the reader visualize the intended result. Furthermore, a more successful goal-setting process is facilitated by the emphasis on ensuring that objectives are favorably phrased and in line with values. Personal development enthusiasts can enhance their goal-setting strategies and cultivate a stronger sense of purpose and accomplishment by incorporating NLP principles.

TIME LINE THERAPY

A keystone of NLP, Time Line Therapy examines how temporal awareness affects a person's behavior and emotional condition. According to this theory, people arrange their experiences in a mental timeline that shapes their feelings and reactions in the present. When it comes to personal growth, Time Line Therapy is an effective method for getting over old traumas, letting go of bad feelings, and cultivating a good outlook. People can take charge of their emotional reactions by using strategies like re-imprinting and timeline visualization, which opens the door to personal development and metamorphosis. Through the application of Time Line Therapy in the framework of NLP, people can liberate themselves from the limitations imposed by their history, promoting emotional stability and resilience.

Examining and changing limiting beliefs that impede personal development is a fundamental component of personal development. NLP offers a methodical way to recognize and get rid of these limiting ideas, allowing people to change the way they think and reach their greatest potential. Through the application of strategies like visualization, belief modification, and reframing, NLP enables people to confront and swap out self-defeating ideas for more empowering ones.

In addition to increasing self-awareness, this technique also acts as a catalyst for personal progress by teaching participants how to approach obstacles with a more upbeat and growth-oriented perspective. By incorporating NLP techniques, individuals can overcome limiting beliefs in a dynamic and transforming journey that leads to a more authentic and fulfilling existence.

SELF-STIMULATION TECHNIQUES

Self-motivation becomes evident in the pursuit of personal development as a crucial component of maintaining advancement and accomplishing long-term objectives. NLP provides a toolkit of techniques to improve self-motivation by utilizing the complex relationship between language, mental processes, and action. A well-known NLP approach called anchoring helps people link happy feelings to particular triggers, which may be a very effective motivational tool. Rephrasing self-defeating thoughts and employing linguistic patterns that bolster motivation are other strategies that help develop a resilient and driven attitude. By incorporating NLP concepts with self-motivation techniques, people can utilize their language and ideas to overcome challenges, maintain focus on their objectives, and encourage a never-ending quest for personal growth.

CHAPTER NINE

USES FOR NATURAL LANGUAGE PROCESSING

NATURAL LANGUAGE PROCESSING (NLP) IN BUSINESS AND LEADERSHIP

NLP has become a very useful tool in business and leadership, transforming how leaders interact and how companies run. NLP is used in business for forecasting market trends, interpreting consumer feedback, and sentiment analysis. This makes it easier for businesses to make data-driven decisions, which helps them stay ahead of the competition.

NLP is used by leaders to improve their ability to understand and adjust to the many communication styles that exist within their teams. NLP also helps with employee engagement by assisting managers in recognizing issues and taking proactive measures to resolve them.

NLP IN THERAPY AND COUNSELING

NLP is a useful tool in the therapeutic and counseling fields for comprehending and changing human behavior. NLP approaches are employed by therapists to recognize and alter thought and behavior patterns, promoting efficient communication and tackling a range of psychological concerns. NLP promotes emotional health and personal development by giving people the tools they need to overcome phobias, limiting beliefs, and traumatic experiences. Therapists can modify therapies according to language patterns, assisting clients in reframing unfavorable ideas and achieving favorable results.

NLP IN EDUCATION

The application of NLP has had a major influence on educational settings. This technology facilitates the creation of automated assessment tools, adaptive learning platforms, and intelligent tutoring systems. NLP analyzes students' natural language interactions to provide individualized learning experiences that are tailored to each student's needs. Sentiment analysis methods can help educators assess the emotional health and level of involvement of their students, allowing for a more comprehensive approach to teaching. Additionally, NLP facilitates applications for language learning, giving students interactive resources for language understanding and acquisition.

NLP INTEGRATION INTO DAILY LIFE

NLP integration into daily life is becoming more and more common, impacting many facets of communication and personal growth. Natural language processing (NLP) improves convenience and productivity in everyday tasks, from intelligent virtual assistants to language translation apps. People can use NLP concepts in interpersonal communication to increase rapport and comprehension. Effective negotiation, persuasion, and conflict resolution can be facilitated by the thoughtful application of linguistic patterns.

Moreover, NLP approaches can be applied to goal-setting and self-improvement, promoting personal development and a positive outlook. NLP technology is expected to become more and more integrated into daily life as it develops, influencing how people interact with one another and with information.

CHAPTER TEN

NLP'S ETHICAL CONSIDERATIONS

NLP PRACTITIONERS' OBLIGATIONS

Natural language processing (NLP) practitioners have a major role in the creation, implementation, and use of NLP technology. Prioritizing the ethical implications of their work while taking into account possible effects on people and society is one of their main responsibilities. Practitioners need to consider how their work might affect security, privacy, and social standards. Important facets of their duties include addressing unexpected repercussions, disclosing any biases, and being transparent in the development process.

Additionally, practitioners must actively participate in continuing education and raising awareness of NLP's ethical issues. It is imperative to remain up to date with the latest ethical standards, industry best practices, and technological developments to guarantee conscientious and long-lasting progress in the domain.

In addition, NLP practitioners have a responsibility to promote moral standards inside their organizations and the larger NLP community by cultivating an environment that values moral judgment.

ASSURING RESPECT AND CONSENT

Getting informed consent is a cornerstone ethical idea in NLP. Before using someone's data, practitioners must make sure they are properly informed about the goals, dangers, and possible ramifications of NLP applications. Transparent communication regarding data collection, storage, and processing procedures is required for this. Furthermore, it's critical to respect users' autonomy and provide them the choice to participate in or not participate in data-gathering operations. Professionals in NLP should give top priority to creating user interfaces that enable transparent and intelligible consent processes.

Another essential component of NLP ethics is respect for tolerance and diversity. To prevent the perpetuation of current socioeconomic disparities, practitioners should actively seek to eliminate biases in training data and algorithms. They also need to be careful when handling concerns like linguistic variances, cultural sensitivity, and the possible negative effects of NLP technologies on underprivileged areas. Promoting moral behavior in the NLP industry requires a dedication to equity and diversity.

NLP AND ETHICS IN DIVERSE SITUATIONS

NLP has ethical ramifications in several fields, including social networking, healthcare, banking, and law enforcement. For example, NLP applications in the healthcare industry need to prioritize patient confidentiality and follow stringent privacy standards. Transparency in algorithmic decision-making is essential to ethical concerns in finance since it guards against discriminatory tactics and guarantees equitable results. NLP technology in law enforcement needs to be used carefully to prevent violating people's civil rights and aggravating preexisting prejudices.

NLP practitioners have to deal with issues like hate speech, misinformation, and privacy violations in the setting of social media. It is a difficult ethical task to strike a balance between content restriction and freedom of expression. NLP technologies ought to be created and applied to improve people's quality of life and society as a whole while reducing harm and upholding moral standards in a variety of settings. To effectively manage these obstacles, practitioners need to be acutely aware of the potential effects that their work may have on individuals, communities, and society at large.

CHAPTER ELEVEN

FUTURE DIRECTIONS FOR NLP

RESEARCH ON NLP HAS ADVANCED

The discipline of natural language processing (NLP) has seen a notable upsurge in study and development in recent years. A significant development is the emergence of transformer-based models, as shown in designs such as GPT-3 and BERT. These models increase language generation and understanding by utilizing attention mechanisms to efficiently capture contextual information. Because of transformers' success, more complex language models have been made possible, which has led to innovation in several NLP tasks, including sentiment analysis, machine translation, and text summarization.

Moreover, there has been interest in the incorporation of multimodal techniques in NLP research. Models that can understand and provide data from both textual and visual inputs are being investigated by researchers.

By adding related images or videos, this method enables NLP systems to comprehend the context of a particular piece of text more fully. The integration of language and vision models presents significant opportunities for applications spanning from enhanced human-computer interactions to content analysis.

EMERGING APPLICATIONS

As NLP technology develops, more and more fields are finding uses for it. The growing application of NLP in healthcare is one noteworthy development. By making it easier to analyze scientific literature, medical texts, and electronic health data, natural language processing promotes more effective information extraction, diagnosis, and decision-making. NLP's capacity to sort through enormous volumes of unstructured data helps to progress clinical research and tailored therapy.

The field of conversational AI and virtual assistants is another developing application. With the use of natural language processing (NLP), chatbots are growing more advanced and can comprehend human intent, have context-aware discussions, and provide more tailored responses. This affects not just customer service but also the creation of virtual assistants and learning resources that adjust to the unique learning preferences of users.

TECHNOLOGY AND NLP

Transformational changes are occurring at the nexus of NLP and technology, impacting multiple industries. Smart speakers and voice-activated systems are increasingly commonplace, demonstrating how NLP is incorporated into daily technology. More conversational and natural interfaces are becoming the norm in human-machine interaction, and natural language processing (NLP) is essential to improving the user experience.

Furthermore, the democratization of NLP technology through pre-trained models and open-source frameworks has sped up its acceptance in a variety of industries. By utilizing pre-trained language models and customizing them for particular applications, developers may now lower entry barriers and promote innovation.

NLP plays a critical role in the big data era by helping to glean valuable insights from enormous textual databases. The enormous volumes of unstructured text data that are produced every day require the management and interpretation of NLP tools, whether they are being used for information extraction for research purposes or sentiment analysis for business intelligence.

The trends for NLP's future point to a sustained development of models, a wide range of applications, and a deeper interaction with different technologies. NLP is positioned to have a significant impact on a wide range of industries, including healthcare, education, and beyond, as research into the area grows. It will shape how people interact with information and technology.